I show I am honest when I

_____

PRECIS ALMANA/PHOTOGRAPH BY MERLE WATERMAN/IMAGERY

_____   _____

name   date

How Many Jawbreakers?

A BOOK ABOUT HONESTY

Terry Thornton
Illustrated by Bartholomew

Chariot Books™
David C. Cook Publishing Co.

Chariot Books™ is an imprint of David C. Cook Publishing Co.
David C. Cook Publishing Co., Elgin, Illinois 60120
David C. Cook Publishing Co., Weston, Ontario
HOW MANY JAWBREAKERS?
© 1990 David C. Cook Publishing Co., Elgin, IL
First Printing, 1990. Printed in the United States of America
94 93 92 91 90 5 4 3 2 1
ISBN 1-55513-967-1 LC 89-60097

The verse marked (TLB) is taken from *The Living Bible* ©1971, owned by assignment by Illinois
Regional Bank N.A. (as trustee). Used by permission of Tyndale House Publishers Inc.,
Wheaton, IL 60189. All rights reserved.

Since the first day of school, a glass jar full of delicious jawbreakers had been sitting on Mrs. Allen's desk. Some lucky person would win that jar and I really hoped it would be me, Andy Jackson.

We were supposed to estimate (that's a fancy word for guess) just how many jawbreakers were in the jar. The boy or girl with the closest estimate would get to keep the jar and the jawbreakers. Mrs. Allen said we would write down our answers this afternoon.

After lunch we went outside to play kickball.
Mrs. Allen forgot her whistle and asked me to go
back and get it.

I ran back to the room and found the whistle
on her desk. Right next to the whistle was a
small note. I turned it around so I could read it. It
said, "732 jawbreakers." I couldn't believe my
luck. It was the answer to the contest!

I grabbed the whistle and rushed out of the room. During the kickball game I kept thinking about the note. I know how many jawbreakers there are. I'm going to win! The jawbreakers will be mine!

Then I started thinking about something else. To write 732 on my paper would be cheating. But I really wanted those jawbreakers. "Jesus," I prayed, "help me do what's right."

After the game we all went back to class. Mrs. Allen said, "OK, boys and girls, this is it. You've used your best estimating skills and have come up with a number. Write down your answer on a sheet of paper. . . ."

I couldn't decide what to do. The jar would be mine—if I cheated. Everyone else was passing their papers forward. Finally, I wrote down 237, just the opposite of the 732 I saw on the note. I was sad that I wouldn't win, but at least I felt good inside knowing that I did what was right. I know Jesus was happy, too.

At last Mrs. Allen said, "I've looked at all your estimates and there were a lot of close ones, but the winner is—oh, wait. Christy had to leave early today, and she left her guess on my desk."

I couldn't believe it! That was the note I saw on the desk.

After looking at Christy's answer, Mrs. Allen said, "There were 232 jawbreakers. The closest estimate was 237 by Andy Jackson. Congratulations, Andy! How did you come up with 237?"

"It was an honest guess, Mrs. Allen. A real honest guess!"